Wheels, wings and water

Aircraft

Lola Schaefer

Raintree

www.raintreepublishers.co.uk
Visit our website to find out more information about **Raintree** books.

To order:
☎ Phone 44 (0) 1865 888112
🗎 Send a fax to 44 (0) 1865 314091
💻 Visit the Heinemann Bookshop at **www.raintreepublishers.co.uk** to browse our catalogue and order online.

First published in Great Britain by Raintree, Halley Court, Jordan Hill, Oxford OX2 8EJ, part of Harcourt Education.
Raintree is a registered trademark of Harcourt Education Ltd.

Editorial: Charlotte Guillain and Diyan Leake
Design: Michelle Lisseter
Picture Research: Maria Joannou and Amor Montes de Oca
Production: Lorraine Hicks

Originated by Dot Gradations
Printed and bound in China by South China Printing Company

ISBN 1 844 21369 2
07 06 05 04 03
10 9 8 7 6 5 4 3 2 1

British Library Cataloguing in Publication Data
Schaefer, Lola
Aircraft. – (Wheels, wings and water)
387.7'3
A full catalogue record for this book is available from the British Library.

Acknowledgements
The publishers would like to thank the following for permission to reproduce photographs: Bruce Coleman, Inc./ Ian & Karen Stewart, 21; Bruce Coleman, Inc./Matt Bradley, 12; Bruce Coleman, Inc./Norman Owen Tomalin, 7, 23 (blade); Corbis/Bettmann, 10; Corbis/Carl & Ann Purcell, 19; Corbis/Charles O'Rear, 4, 23 (vehicle); Corbis/Museum of Flight, 11; Corbis/Patrick Bennett, 9; Corbis/Philip Wallick, 15, 22, 24, backcover; Corbis/Richard Hamilton Smith, 18; Corbis/Richard T. Nowitz, 20, 23 (skis); Visuals Unlimited/A&E Morris, 6; Visuals Unlimited/Arthur Morris, 16; Visuals Unlimited/ Bruce Berg, 14, 23 (engine), backcover; Visuals Unlimited/ Jeffrey Greenberg, 13; Visuals Unlimited/Jeffrey Howe, 5, 17, 23 (propeller); Visuals Unlimited/Swartzell, 8

Cover photograph of helicopter, reproduced with permission of Tudor Photography.

Every effort has been made to contact copyright holders of any material reproduced in this book. Any omissions will be rectified in subsequent printings if notice is given to the publishers.

Some words are shown in bold, **like this**. You can find them in the glossary on page 23.

Contents

What are aircraft?

Aircraft are **vehicles** that fly.

They carry people or things in the air.

propeller

engine

Engines and **propellers** make some aircraft fly.

Some aircraft use hot air, gas or wind to move.

What do aircraft look like?

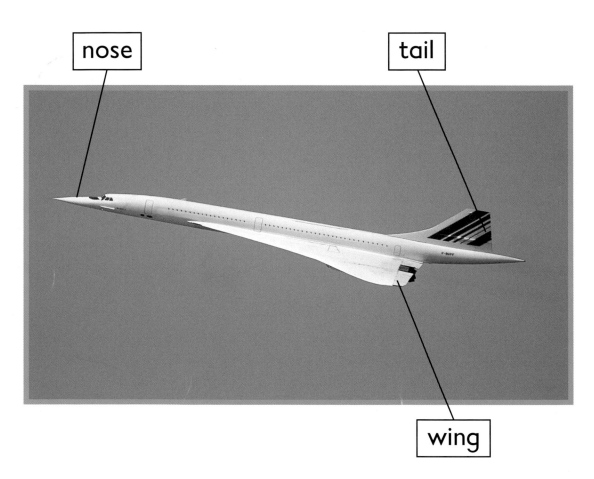

nose

tail

wing

Most aircraft have two wings, a tail and a nose.

This aeroplane looks like a big bird!

blades

Some aircraft do not have wings.

This helicopter has **blades** instead.

What are aircraft made of?

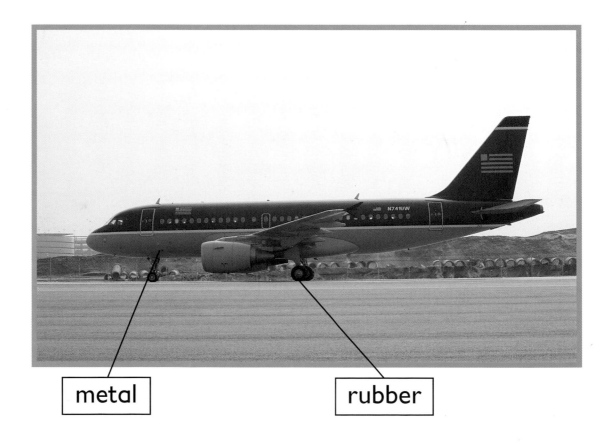

metal

rubber

The outsides of most aircraft are metal.

Tyres are made of rubber.

plastic

cloth

The seats in most aircraft are cloth.

Some parts are made of plastic.

How did aircraft look in the past?

The first aircraft were made of wood, cloth and wire.

People who flew them sat on poles.

After that, aeroplanes were made of metal.

They had windows and doors.

What is an aeroplane?

An aeroplane is an aircraft
with wings.

Some aeroplanes are very small.

Aeroplanes can be big, too.

They can carry many people.

What is a jet?

engine

A jet is an aeroplane without **propellers**.

A jet's **engines** are more powerful than propellers.

Jets can fly very high in the sky.

They are fast, too!

What is a helicopter?

blades

Helicopters are aircraft with **blades** instead of **propellers**.

An **engine** turns the blades.

Helicopters can fly up, down
or sideways.

They can even stay still in the air.

What is an airship?

An airship is a large balloon filled with a light gas.

The gas makes the airship go up.

An **engine** moves the airship through the air.

Airships can only carry a few people.

Why are some aircraft special?

ski

Seaplanes are aircraft that take off and land on water.

They float on two long **skis**.

basket

Hot-air balloons carry people in a basket.

Hot air lifts the balloon into the air.

Quiz

Do you know what kind of aircraft this is?

Can you find it in the book?

Look for the answer on page 24.

Glossary

blade
long, thin flat object with sharp edges, like the turning blades on a helicopter

engine
machine that makes a vehicle move

propeller
specially shaped blades that turn very fast to power an aeroplane or a ship

skis
long, thin pieces of plastic, wood or metal used to move over snow or water

vehicle
machine that carries people or things from place to place

Index

Answer to quiz on page 22.
This is a jet.

Titles in the Wheels, Wings and Water series include:

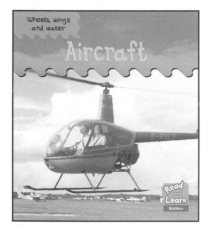

Hardback   1 844 21369 2

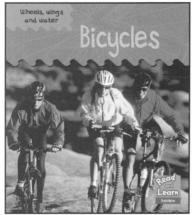

Hardback   1 844 21371 4

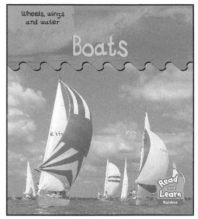

Hardback   1 844 21366 8

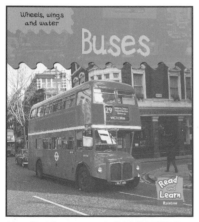

Hardback   1 844 21373 0

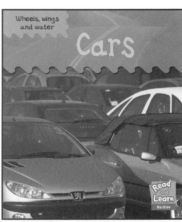

Hardback   1 844 21372 2

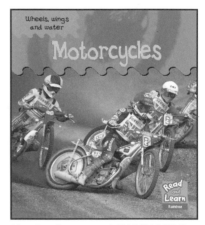

Hardback   1 844 21367 6

Hardback   1 844 21368 4

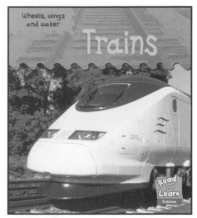

Hardback   1 844 21374 9

Find out about the other titles in this series on our website www.raintreepublishers.co.uk